AF422807

the mighty tecumseh for kids

Warrior and Peacemaker

sarah michaels

Copyright © 2024 by Sarah Michaels

All rights reserved.

No part of this book may be reproduced in any form or by any electronic or mechanical means, including information storage and retrieval systems, without written permission from the author, except for the use of brief quotations in a book review.

contents

1 /
the early years

introduction to tecumseh

IMAGINE STANDING at the edge of a vast forest, the leaves whispering secrets of the past and the ground beneath your feet echoing with the footsteps of many who walked before you. In the heart of such a forest, over two centuries ago, lived a boy who would grow up to be one of the most remarkable leaders in American history. His name was Tecumseh, which means "shooting star," and just like a bright light racing across the night sky, his story is swift, brilliant, and unforgettable.

Tecumseh was born into the Shawnee tribe during a time of great change and challenge. The Shawnee people, like many other Native American tribes, were deeply connected to the land they lived on. They believed that the earth was a gift to everyone, and no single person could own it like one might own a pair of moccasins or a wooden bowl. This belief was central to Tecumseh's life and later became a cornerstone of his vision.

As a young boy, Tecumseh's playground was the lush landscapes of what is now Ohio. He learned to hunt and fish, moving silently through the dense forests, listening to the wind, and understanding the language of nature. But Tecumseh's childhood was not just filled with play; it was also a time of learning about the struggles his people faced. Settlers from European countries were moving westward across North America, claiming land as their own and pushing Tecumseh's tribe and many others from their homes.

These were hard lessons for a young heart, but Tecumseh grew from them. He saw the need for strength and unity among his people. As he grew into a young man, he became known not just for his skills as a hunter and warrior but for his ability to lead and inspire. He had a powerful presence and when he spoke, his words could stir the heart of anyone who listened.

Tecumseh's dream was bold and big. He wanted to unite all Native American tribes into a single confederation, a group strong enough to protect their homes, their way of life, and their future. He believed that if all the tribes worked together, they could resist the settlers and live on their lands as they always had. This dream was not just about stopping the settlers; it was about respecting the sacredness of the earth and living in harmony with it.

Traveling far and wide, Tecumseh met with leaders from different tribes. From the deep woods of the east to the great plains west of the Mississippi, he shared his vision, urging unity and courage. His passion and sincerity won him many followers and friends. However, this path was not without its dangers and challenges. Not everyone agreed with Tecumseh's ideas, and the world around him was changing rapidly.

Despite these challenges, Tecumseh never wavered. His belief in the power of unity and the importance of protecting the land guided him through countless negotiations and conflicts. His journey was not just about battles and speeches; it was also about building a legacy of respect, courage, and commitment to a cause greater than oneself.

Tecumseh's life is a tapestry of thrilling adventures, heartfelt speeches, and unyielding dedication. As we explore his story, we'll see not just the battles he fought but also understand why he fought them. We'll learn about the friendships he forged, the hardships he endured, and the unwavering vision that guided him like a star through the darkest nights.

Now, let's journey back in time and walk alongside Tecumseh, the shooting star. Let's watch as he grows from a young boy, curious and brave, into a leader whose name would echo through history, inspiring many who believe in the power of unity and the sanctity of their homeland.

childhood

Imagine stirring from your slumber to the early sunshine filtering through the giant oaks that towered overhead, the cool scent of the ground and wildflowers filling the air. This was Tecumseh's world, a young Shawnee boy named after a shooting star who would one day grow up to be revered as a great leader. His boyhood played out on the rolling hills of the Ohio Valley, a place where the weather and the seasons decided the pace of living every day.

Tecumseh was born into a loving family, part of a larger community that valued cooperation, respect, and the bonds of kinship. His father was a respected warrior and his mother a wise and caring figure in the tribe. From them, Tecumseh learned the importance of family and community ties, lessons that would shape his vision and leadership in later years.

In the Shawnee tribe, children were cherished. They were considered gifts from the Creator, meant to be nurtured and taught with care. Tecumseh and his siblings spent their days playing near the streams and forests, learning to appreciate the abundance of nature that surrounded them. These playgrounds were not just spaces for fun, but classrooms where life's most important lessons were taught.

From a very young age, Tecumseh learned to listen to the wind, to understand the language of birds, and to know the healing powers of plants. His mother taught him how to gather herbs and his father took him on long walks, pointing out the tracks of deer and the dens of foxes. These lessons were about more than survival; they were about living in harmony with the world around them.

The Shawnee people moved with the seasons, setting up camps by the rivers in the summer and moving to the protection of the forests during the colder months. Tecumseh's family was always busy. Spring was for planting, summer for fishing and gathering, autumn for hunting, and winter for storytelling by the fire. Each season brought its own joys and challenges, and Tecumseh grew up understanding the cycle of life and the importance of adapting to change.

Meals were a communal affair, a time for sharing not only food but stories and songs as well. Tecumseh learned the art of storytelling from his elders, who passed down tales of Shawnee heroes and the history of their people. These stories were like seeds planted in his young mind, growing into a deep love for his culture and a fierce pride in his heritage.

As Tecumseh grew, so did his responsibilities. By the age of ten, he was learning to use a bow and arrow, to fish with spears, and to canoe across the swift rivers. These skills were important for his survival, but they were also a way to contribute to his family and community. Tecumseh was taught that every member of the tribe had a role to play, and that working together was the key to their collective well-being.

The natural environment was a constant source of wonder for Tecumseh. He watched the stars wheel across the sky at night and learned to read the weather from the clouds. He felt a deep connection to the land, which was viewed not as a resource to be exploited, but as a living, breathing entity to be respected and protected.

This connection to the land and his community's way of life shaped Tecumseh's early years. He saw the beauty of his world and the wisdom of his people's way of life, but he also noticed the shadows that were falling across their land. Settlers were encroaching, and tensions were rising. These were serious concerns, but in his youth, they were background worries, whispers among the adults after the children had gone to sleep.

During Tecumseh's childhood, the components of life for him were like a weaved mat made from family, community, and nature. Each experience was a lesson; each lesson was a stepping stone toward his destiny. As Tecumseh grew older, he learned the values of respecting the earth, love for his people, and togetherness coined as unity, that would help push him into leadership at a young age in difficult times.

formative events

As seasons advanced, and Tecumseh grew taller, the natural world about him began to change in ways that were much more difficult to interpret than the arrival and departure of frost. It was a time when Shawnee and other tribal lands were becoming the battleground for much greater powers than any single tribe. Indeed, it was the era of the American Revolution, when American colonists were fighting for independence from British rule, a struggle that would eventually prove life-changing for Tecumseh and his people.

Tecumseh was just a boy when the echoes of this great conflict reached the Shawnee. Although the fight was primarily between the colonists and the British, Native American tribes found themselves caught in the middle. Some sided with the British, hoping that a British victory would stop the colonists from pushing further into their lands. Others sided with the Americans, encouraged by promises of peace and land protection. Tecumseh's tribe, the Shawnee, found themselves divided on where to stand.

During these tumultuous times, Tecumseh witnessed first-hand the impacts of war. His father, Puckeshinwa, was a warrior who joined forces with those who supported the British. The ideals of bravery and loyalty that his father embodied were not lost on young Tecumseh, who admired his father's courage. Tragically, his father would not return from the fighting, leaving Tecumseh's family to face the future without him. This loss marked a turning point for Tecumseh, etching into his heart a deep sorrow but also igniting a fierce determination.

With the absence of his father, the responsibility of helping his family fell more heavily on Tecumseh's shoulders. He learned that leadership was not just about guiding others in times of peace but also about holding them together in times of hardship. The stories of his father's bravery became a beacon for Tecumseh, who now saw the importance of protecting his people and their way of life.

As the American Revolution raged on, the Shawnee and other tribes experienced increasing pressure. The settlers, fueled by their newfound independence and expanding visions, pushed further into Native American territories. This encroachment brought frequent clashes, as Native American tribes defended their lands against settlers who were often indifferent to the long-standing ties the tribes had to the land.

Tecumseh watched as treaties were made and broken, and as promises turned into disappointments. These were his formative lessons in diplomacy and betrayal. He saw tribal leaders struggle to find the right path, some choosing peace at any cost, and others fighting to preserve their lands and sovereignty. Through these experiences, Tecumseh learned the complex dance of negotiation and the harsh realities of power dynamics.

Despite the turmoil, Tecumseh's connection to his heritage and the teachings of his elders remained firm. He learned about the Great Law of Peace, an ancient code that governed interactions among various tribes with respect and fairness. These principles profoundly shaped his thinking about leadership and justice. They taught him that true strength lay in unity and that peace was not simply the absence of war but a profound respect for all beings.

Tecumseh also experienced the power of story-telling during this time, as oral histories and tribal legends served not just to entertain but to educate and preserve the culture. He understood that stories could unite people, kindle their spirits, and guide them through darkness. This understanding would later become central to his efforts to unite diverse tribes under a common cause.

As Tecumseh stepped into adolescence, the scars of the American Revolution began to shape a new landscape in his homeland. The war had ended with the Treaty of Paris, but peace did not return to the lands of the Shawnee. Instead, the floodgates opened for settlers driven by a desire for land and expansion. For Tecumseh, these events steeled his resolve. The young boy who had once roamed the forests and listened to the stories of his ancestors now saw a clear vision of his path. He would stand for his people, fight for their rights, and strive for a unity that could protect them against any force.

Through these formative years, the seeds of leadership were sown in Tecumseh's heart. Each event, each story, each loss, and each victory watered these seeds, preparing him to become the leader he needed to be—a leader not just for a battle but for a greater cause that would echo through the generations. As we move forward in his story, we see not just a young man shaped by events but a visionary who would rise to meet the challenges of a changing world.

becoming a leader

learning to lead

AS TECUMSEH GREW from a boy into a young man, his heart and mind were filled with lessons learned from the land, his people, and the stories of his ancestors. Each step he took through the forests of his homeland not only connected him deeper to the earth but also to the responsibilities that lay ahead. Tecumseh's path to leadership began not with a grand event, but through small moments that taught him about courage, wisdom, and the importance of unity.

After the loss of his father, Tecumseh's family looked to him for strength and guidance. Though he was still young, the weight of expectation rested on his shoulders. His first test as a leader came unexpectedly during a hunting trip. Tecumseh, leading a small group of younger boys, needed to ensure they all returned home safely. When a sudden storm swept through the valley, blocking their path with rushing waters and making the woods a maze of shadows, Tecumseh remembered the calm voice of his father during similar storms. He kept his group calm, found shelter, and managed to navigate back home using the natural signs his father had taught him. This experience taught him the first rule of leadership: the welfare of the group depends on calm and decisive actions.

As Tecumseh's reputation for maturity and thoughtfulness grew, so did the opportunities for him to lead. He was invited to listen in on council meetings, where tribal elders debated issues ranging from land disputes to alliance proposals. Here, Tecumseh learned his second lesson of leadership: the power of listening. He noticed that the most respected leaders were not just those who spoke well, but those who listened, learned, and then led.

. . .

Tecumseh's first major challenge as a leader came when he was a teenager, during a negotiation with a neighboring tribe over hunting grounds. The discussions were tense, with the threat of conflict looming large. Tecumseh remembered the stories of his ancestors, who spoke of peace and unity as strengths. He proposed a shared use of the land, a novel idea that required both tribes to hunt responsibly and respect each other's needs. This proposal showed his understanding of compromise and his commitment to peace, marking his emergence as a thoughtful leader among his people.

With each passing year, Tecumseh's influence grew, but so did the challenges he faced. Settlers continued to encroach on Shawnee lands, and the promises made by the American government were often broken. Tecumseh saw the impact of these broken promises on his people, and it drove him to a deeper commitment. He began to travel, meeting with leaders of other tribes, sharing his vision of a united Native American front. His charisma and sincerity attracted followers, but his message also brought challenges, as not everyone believed in his vision of unity.

. . .

Tecumseh's leadership was not just about speaking and negotiating. It was also about setting an example. He hunted with the young men of his tribe, sharing techniques and stories. He discussed the teachings of the Great Law of Peace with the children, instilling in them the values of respect and harmony. Through these actions, Tecumseh demonstrated another key aspect of leadership: teaching by doing.

The true test of Tecumseh's leadership came as he began to form what would be known as the Tecumseh Confederacy, an alliance of Native American tribes united against American expansion. This was not just a military alliance but a profound cultural and social movement. Tecumseh preached not only resistance but also a return to traditional ways, away from the influence of European settlers. His vision was of a united Native American identity, strong and free from the divisions that had weakened them in the past.

As Tecumseh traveled from tribe to tribe, he faced skepticism and hostility as well as support. He learned to negotiate, persuade, and inspire. Each encounter sharpened his skills and deepened his understanding of the diverse perspectives within different tribes. His relentless dedication to his cause earned him respect, even among those who initially doubted him.

As Tecumseh rose to leadership, he had setbacks as well as victories, and each experience taught him different lessons about leading a diverse group toward a common objective. He came to understand that leadership was not about forcing people to do what the leader wanted, but more about how to weave the many separate strands of society together to make a unit.

vision for unity

A vision began to emerge to Tecumseh as he looked out over the expansive forests and undulating plains that he thought of as home. This vision was a powerful one that could bring together the many distinct groups of people into one common cause. The essence of his vision was not about gaining power, but instead was based on deep love for his people and place . It was about connecting Native American tribes together so they could resist the European settlers who were entering their lands.

• • •

Tecumseh had seen the divisions among the tribes, how these divisions made them vulnerable to the pressures and tactics of the settlers. He knew that if these tribes continued to act alone, they would be overpowered one by one. But together, united as one body, they could present a formidable resistance, protecting their lands and their ways of life. This was Tecumseh's goal—to forge a coalition of tribes that would operate as a single, powerful entity.

The journey to realize this vision began with Tecumseh sharing his thoughts with his own people, the Shawnee. He spoke passionately about the strength in unity and the dangers of division. His words were like seeds, planted in the hearts of those who heard him, and they began to take root. But Tecumseh knew that talking to his tribe alone was not enough. He needed to reach out to other tribes, to convince them to join his cause.

Armed with nothing but his convictions and his oratory skills, Tecumseh set out on a series of journeys that would take him far from his homeland. He traveled across vast distances, from the deep woods of the north to the sun-scorched lands of the south, meeting with tribal leaders, warriors, and elders. At each stop, he shared his vision of a united front against the settlers, speaking of a confederacy that could protect all their futures.

Tecumseh's arguments were persuasive because they came from a place of deep sincerity and an evident understanding of the threats they all faced. He spoke about how the settlers' ways were different, how they saw land as something to own and to use for profit, rather than something to live with in harmony. He talked about the settlers' relentless push into Native territories, their disregard for the treaties they signed, and the diseases they brought with them, which decimated tribes.

His message was clear: alone, each tribe might fall, but together, they could stand strong. He reminded the tribes of their ancient connections, their shared stories, and their common heritage. He urged them not only to think of their immediate families but of the generations yet to come. Would those children and grandchildren inherit lands stripped of their resources, or would they know the bounty of a well-protected earth?

As Tecumseh spoke, he listened too. He understood that each tribe had its concerns and priorities. Some were weary of war, having faced losses too great to bear. Others were skeptical of joining forces with tribes they had previously seen as rivals. Tecumseh's leadership shone through in these moments. He acknowledged their fears, he respected their losses, and he sought to weave their different perspectives into the larger tapestry of his vision.

With each tribe that agreed to join his confederacy, the dream of unity grew stronger. Tecumseh and his allies worked to create a sense of brotherhood among these diverse groups. They held gatherings where members from different tribes could meet, share stories, and participate in cultural exchanges. These gatherings were not just political meetings but celebrations of a shared identity and common cause.

• • •

The challenges were immense. Not every tribe was convinced, and not every leader was willing to commit. Tecumseh faced setbacks and disappointments, but his resolve did not waver. He continued to travel, to speak, and to build alliances. His reputation as a leader and a visionary spread, and his confederacy began to take shape.

This confederacy was not just a military alliance but a cultural revival. Tecumseh urged the tribes to return to their traditional ways, to forsake the goods and the influences of the European settlers. He preached self-reliance, respect for tradition, and a renewed commitment to the spiritual practices that had guided his ancestors.

Tecumseh's vision for unity was a beacon that called to many, a dream of a powerful confederacy that could change the course of history for Native American peoples. His dedication to this dream, his ability to inspire and to lead, and his unwavering commitment to the welfare of all Native peoples carved his place in history as one of the most remarkable leaders of his time.

3 /

the call to action

building alliances

THE DREAM of uniting Native American tribes under a single cause set Tecumseh on a path far wider and more winding than the rivers of his homeland. His mission was to gather different tribes into a powerful confederacy that could stand against the relentless tide of European settlers. This chapter of Tecumseh's life is a journey across vast distances, through diverse cultures, and amidst varying beliefs of Native American tribes across what is now the United States.

Armed with his vision of unity, Tecumseh began his travels, stepping into the role of a diplomat as much as a leader. His first destination was often a neighboring tribe with whom the Shawnee had longstanding relations. But as his ambition grew, so did his reach, extending to tribes far beyond his familiar territories.

Each meeting with a new tribe was both a challenge and an opportunity. Tecumseh knew that the success of his mission depended not only on his ability to communicate his vision but also on his ability to listen and adapt to the concerns and conditions of each tribe. Every tribe had its own experiences with settlers, its own losses, and victories, and its own cultural nuances. Tecumseh approached each tribe with respect, acknowledging their sovereignty and the value of their traditions.

Imagine Tecumseh, standing in a council meeting with the leaders of the Creek tribe in the deep South. Here, he spoke not only of the threats from settlers but also of the potential for trade and support among the tribes. He discussed military strategies, drawing from his knowledge of European tactics and Shawnee warfare. Tecumseh's rhetoric was impassioned yet grounded in practicality. He spoke of a united front that could offer mutual protection and benefit, appealing to the leaders' sense of duty to their people.

In the northern woods, among the Great Lakes tribes, Tecumseh's approach shifted. Here, he emphasized the spiritual and cultural connections between the tribes, invoking shared legends and prophetic visions that spoke of a united Native American force. He used the commonalities in their spiritual beliefs to weave a narrative of unity, suggesting that their combined strength was foretold by their ancestors.

Tecumseh's journeys also took him to the far west, among tribes that had experienced less direct contact with settlers. With these tribes, he often faced skepticism about the scale of the threat he described. To persuade them, Tecumseh shared stories of tribes displaced from their lands, of battles lost and pyrrhic victories. His stories were vivid and heartfelt, carrying the emotional weight of personal experience.

As Tecumseh traveled, he adapted his message to each audience, but his core message remained the same: unity was their best defense against the settlers. This was a complex conversation to have, involving not just political and military considerations but also deep cultural and spiritual elements. Tecumseh's ability to navigate these complex conversations was a testament to his leadership and his profound commitment to his cause.

But Tecumseh's mission was not without its setbacks. While many leaders were moved by his vision and charisma, others were reluctant to join a pan-tribal alliance. Some were wary of losing their autonomy; others doubted the feasibility of such a grand coalition. Each refusal was a blow, but Tecumseh remained undeterred, learning from each encounter and refining his approach.

Accompanying Tecumseh on many of these journeys was his brother, Tenskwatawa, known as the Prophet, who added a spiritual dimension to Tecumseh's diplomatic efforts. Tenskwatawa's visions and religious messages provided a spiritual context to the political and military alliance Tecumseh proposed. Together, the brothers made a compelling pair, blending the practical with the prophetic.

Throughout these travels, Tecumseh also faced immense personal risks. Traveling through unfamiliar territories, often in harsh conditions, tested his endurance and commitment. Yet, these hardships only sharpened his resolve, fueling his dedication to the cause.

Tecumseh's travels and efforts to build alliances were about more than forming a military coalition; they were about fostering a sense of broader community among the tribes. He envisioned a confederacy that could not only resist settler expansion but also revitalize the cultural and spiritual bonds among the tribes, reminding them of their shared heritage and interlinked destinies.

This quest to build alliances was a defining period in Tecumseh's life. It showed his unparalleled dedication to his people and his unique ability to unify diverse groups under a common cause.

obstacles and challenges

Tecumseh's attempt to unite the native tribes was marked by a blend of triumph and failure. He had the grand idea and the forceful leadership, but the journey was full of challenge. The challenges were not just the division of the tribes themselves, but the opposition of European Americans. Each move he made brought new troubles and tested his strength and the heart of his idea.

One of the first and most persistent challenges Tecumseh faced was skepticism from within some of the tribes he visited. While many admired his eloquence and passion, not all were ready to join his confederacy. Some tribal leaders were cautious, worried about losing their independence and the autonomy of their tribes. They feared that aligning with other tribes under a single leader might dilute their own authority and the traditions unique to their people. Tecumseh had to navigate these delicate political waters carefully, respecting each tribe's individuality while emphasizing the greater good that could come from unity.

Furthermore, there were disagreements over strategy. Some leaders preferred peaceful tactics, hoping to secure their lands through treaties and negotiations. Others had already faced betrayals and were skeptical of any approach that relied on dialogue with settlers. Tecumseh, however, knew that their combined strength was necessary for any resistance to be effective, whether it involved negotiation or defense. He worked tirelessly to find common ground, often spending days with a single tribe, discussing and debating until a consensus could be reached.

External political pressures also posed significant challenges. The United States government was expanding its territory, and with each new state added to the Union, more land was taken from Native tribes. The government often employed tactics that sowed division among tribes, offering individual treaties to different groups, which undermined Tecumseh's efforts to promote collective action. These treaties were frequently unfair, poorly understood by the tribes due to language barriers, or outright deceptive.

Additionally, the ever-changing political landscape of the United States presented a moving target. Tecumseh had to keep abreast of U.S. politics, understanding shifts in policy and leadership, which could abruptly change the circumstances for his people. This required not only intelligence and foresight but also flexibility in strategy and alliances.

Another profound challenge was the internal conflict between tribes that had historical grievances against each other. Centuries-old conflicts over land, resources, or slights had created deep-seated mistrust between some communities. Tecumseh found himself not only a leader and a diplomat but also a mediator, trying to heal old wounds to foster a new sense of brotherhood among the tribes.

Tecumseh's younger brother, Tenskwatawa, known as the Prophet, added both strength and complication to Tecumseh's efforts. The Prophet's spiritual message resonated with many, but his forceful, sometimes radical approaches to cultural revival and rejection of European influences were polarizing. While Tecumseh saw his brother's religious leadership as integral to uniting the tribes under shared spiritual values, it occasionally alienated those who were less inclined toward radical change.

Despite these myriad challenges, Tecumseh's determination did not waver. He believed deeply in the possibility of a united Native front, and each setback only strengthened his resolve. He adapted his strategies, sometimes offering military aid to tribes in immediate conflict with settlers or the U.S. military, at other times providing economic assistance to foster goodwill and mutual dependence.

Tecumseh's leadership during this period was a balancing act of extraordinary complexity. He had to be a warrior and a peacemaker, a politician and a brother. He traveled extensively, spoke tirelessly, and dreamed passionately of a future where all Native peoples could live in security and sovereignty on their ancestral lands.

4 /
the war of 1812

tecumseh and the war

AS THE EARLY 19th century unfolded, tensions in America were not just simmering; they were boiling. The young United States found itself embroiled in conflicts both within its borders and with external powers. This was the setting for the War of 1812, a complex conflict involving the United States, Britain, and various Native American tribes. Tecumseh, a formidable leader with a vision of unity among Native tribes, played a pivotal role in this tumultuous chapter of history.

Tecumseh's involvement in the War of 1812 was not just a matter of circumstance; it was a strategic choice. The war provided an opportunity to push back against American expansionism, which threatened the lands and the ways of life of the Native peoples. Tecumseh saw an alliance with the British as a means to an end—the protection of Native territories from American settlers.

The alliance with the British was tactical. Britain, still smarting from losing its American colonies, was not averse to supporting Native American efforts that could destabilize the United States. For Tecumseh, the British offered supplies, arms, and, most importantly, a partnership that could potentially help achieve a significant halt to American westward expansion.

One of the first major engagements in which Tecumseh played a crucial role was the Siege of Detroit. In this battle, Tecumseh and his force of Native warriors teamed up with British Major General Isaac Brock to confront American forces. Tecumseh's tactical acumen and his warriors' fierce determination proved instrumental in the British and Native American forces' surprising victory. Tecumseh's strategy involved a clever ruse that made the American forces believe they were facing a much larger Native force than was actually present, leading to a swift and decisive British victory without significant bloodshed.

However, the alliance with the British was not without its challenges. Tecumseh found himself frequently frustrated by the constraints of cooperating with British military tactics and their diplomatic considerations. He was a warrior used to leading his men directly, guided by the immediate needs of his people and the fluid dynamics of Native warfare. The British, however, operated under a different set of military doctrines and political constraints, which sometimes led to missed opportunities and frustrating delays.

Despite these challenges, Tecumseh remained a steadfast leader. He rallied a confederation of tribes who fought valiantly in several key battles throughout the war. One such battle was the Battle of the Thames, where Tecumseh's leadership would once again be on full display. In this pivotal conflict, despite being outnumbered and facing a well-equipped American army, Tecumseh's forces fought with the courage and ferocity that were his trademark.

Tragically, it was in this battle that Tecumseh would fall, his life cut short by an American bullet. The loss of Tecumseh was not just a military blow but a deep, symbolic loss for the Native American resistance. His death marked a turning point in the war and in the hopes of many Native tribes for a united resistance against American expansion.

Tecumseh's role in the War of 1812 is a story of

bravery, strategic genius, and profound leadership. It highlights his ability to see beyond immediate battles to the broader implications of the struggle for Native lands and rights. His alliances were not just military tactics; they were part of a larger vision that sought to secure a future for his people and other tribes. Tecumseh's legacy in this conflict is a testament to his skills as a leader and a warrior but also to his deep commitment to the survival and sovereignty of Native American peoples.

His efforts during the War of 1812 exemplify how he was able to adapt to new alliances and the changing landscape of power, all while maintaining his integrity and focus on the larger goals of protection and unity among Native tribes. Though the war did not end in favor of the Native Americans, Tecumseh's impact was indelible, leaving a legacy that would inspire generations to come.

heroism and strategy

Some figures stand out for their sheer force of will, their courage, and their keen minds. Tecumseh, a leader of the Shawnee and a visionary who dreamed of unity, was one such figure. His life was a series of battles—not just physical conflicts but also strategic confrontations where he used his intellect and bravery to fight for his people's future.

One of the most telling moments of Tecumseh's heroism and strategic acumen was during the Siege of Fort Meigs. Here, Tecumseh and his warriors, alongside their British allies, faced American forces in a significant standoff. Tecumseh's role was not only to lead his warriors in battle but also to strategize alongside British commanders. It was here that Tecumseh demonstrated his profound understanding of both traditional Native American warfare and European military tactics.

During the siege, Tecumseh devised a plan to lure the American forces into a trap. He knew the land well—every hill, river, and valley—a knowledge he used to his advantage. Tecumseh sent a small group of warriors to feign a retreat through a narrow passage, enticing the American soldiers to follow. The passage led to a hidden encampment where Tecumseh and the bulk of his forces waited. The plan was set, and as the American troops followed the retreating warriors, Tecumseh's forces surrounded them. The battle that ensued was fierce, and though the siege itself stretched on without a clear victory, Tecumseh's trap led to heavy losses for the American forces, showcasing his strategic brilliance.

Another significant moment in Tecumseh's military career was during the Battle of Tippecanoe. Although ultimately a defeat for Tecumseh's confederacy, the battle displayed Tecumseh's foresight and tactical intelligence. Before the battle, Tecumseh had traveled widely to forge alliances with various tribes, and he planned to unite them in a grand coalition. His strategy was to amass enough strength to repel the American settlers and soldiers gradually encroaching on Native lands. The battle itself, led in Tecumseh's absence by his brother, Tenskwatawa, did not go as planned, but it underscored the importance of Tecumseh's leadership and vision. His preparations, the alliances he formed, and his plans laid the groundwork for what could have been a pivotal resistance had he been there to lead his forces personally.

Tecumseh's strategies often included psychological elements designed to intimidate or deceive his opponents. For example, Tecumseh was known for his ability to manipulate the perceptions of his enemies. During negotiations or prior to battles, he would orchestrate impressive displays of force, having his warriors parade repeatedly through a clearing in the woods to appear as a much larger army to spies or scouts watching from a distance. This tactic of psychological intimidation made his forces seem more formidable and often gave the enemy pause, buying Tecumseh crucial time to strengthen his position or prepare for an attack.

The most profound testament to Tecumseh's bravery came during the Battle of the Thames, where he met his heroic end. As the battle grew desperate, Tecumseh was seen rallying his warriors, refusing to retreat, even as the odds turned starkly against him. He rode back and forth, a striking figure, urging his warriors to stand firm and fight with honor for the land that was rightfully theirs. His leadership in that final battle was emblematic of his entire life's dedication to his people and their sovereignty.

Tecumseh's death in battle did not just mark the end of a life; it symbolized the culmination of a lifetime of leadership, bravery, and strategic genius. He had spent years weaving together a confederacy of diverse tribes, each with its own customs and grievances, into a unified force capable of challenging the expanding American frontier.

5 /
tecumseh's legacy

the end of his journey

IN THE WEAVE of American history, few threads are as vibrant and striking as Tecumseh, whose life exemplified the struggles of freedom and justice. His last stand at the Thames was not only the end of his life journey but also the commencement of his enduring legacy.

Tecumseh's life ended in 1813 during the Battle of the Thames, where he fought valiantly against American forces. While his death marked the end of his efforts to unite the Native American tribes against encroaching settlers, it did not erase the impacts of his actions, which resonated far beyond the battlefields.

After his death, Tecumseh's vision of a unified Native resistance slowly unraveled. Without his leadership and unifying presence, the confederacy of tribes began to dissipate. Many returned to their lands, facing renewed pressures from settlers and the government. However, the dream Tecumseh had kindled did not die entirely. His courage and conviction inspired future generations to continue the struggle for Native rights and sovereignty. Tecumseh had shown what could be possible when different tribes worked together toward a common goal.

Tecumseh's strategic mind and diplomatic prowess also left a significant mark on military and leadership studies. He is often studied as a model of indigenous leadership who combined traditional warrior skills with keen strategic insights. His tactics during battles, such as the Siege of Detroit and the Battle of Tippecanoe, are noted for their innovative use of both psychological warfare and intimate knowledge of terrain.

Beyond his military and political achievements, Tecumseh's legacy is also preserved in the way he influenced cultural identity among Native American tribes. He advocated for a return to traditional values and practices, resisting the cultural assimilation pushed by American settlers. His stance helped sow seeds of cultural pride and revitalization that would grow in the centuries that followed, reminding his people of the importance of heritage and identity.

Tecumseh's impact also extended into the broader narrative of American history. He became a symbol of resistance against injustice and a hero not only to Native Americans but to all who value freedom and respect for diverse cultures. His efforts to protect his people and their lands from external domination resonated with other minority groups and those facing oppression, making his story a rallying cry for resilience and resistance.

Educationally, Tecumseh's life and legacy are often highlighted in school curriculums to help young students understand the complex history of Native American interactions with European settlers. Through books, documentaries, and classroom discussions, children learn about Tecumseh's role in American history, his leadership qualities, and his vision for his people, sparking conversations about justice, leadership, and the consequences of colonization.

Monuments and historical sites also commemorate Tecumseh's life and battles, serving as physical reminders of his contributions and the profound costs of the conflicts between Native Americans and European settlers. These sites are places of reflection and education, where visitors can learn about the historical context of Tecumseh's life and the ongoing challenges faced by Native American communities.

Tecumseh's story continues to inspire works of art, literature, and performance, capturing the imagination of creators who see in his story themes of heroism, tragedy, and the eternal struggle for justice. Plays, poems, and novels recount his life and times, each interpretation exploring different facets of his character and his quest.

As we recount the story of Tecumseh's life, from his humble beginnings to his final days as a leader of a grand confederacy, we see a figure larger than life, yet deeply human. Tecumseh's journey through this world was a quest not just for land or power but for the very survival of a way of life that he held sacred. His end was a testament to his unwavering dedication to his people and their right to live freely on their ancestral lands.

Tecumseh's legacy is not just in the battles he fought but in the spirit of hope and resistance he instilled—a legacy that continues to teach and inspire.

tecumseh's influence today

Despite the fact that it is more than two centuries since Tecumseh's birth, his influence and legacy feel very current. He was a great figure who played many roles, but was also a great leader who understood the importance of unity and the sacredness of the natural world. The values Tecumseh shared are very relevant for us today, as we face a number of global crises.

Tecumseh's belief in unity among diverse groups provides a powerful lesson in today's world, where division often seems more common than agreement. He dreamed of bringing together Native American tribes of various backgrounds and languages to stand united in protecting their lands and way of life. This idea of unity can inspire us today, reminding us that by working together, we can overcome great obstacles. Schools across the country teach Tecumseh's history not just to explore the past, but to show how collaboration and respect for different cultures are essential in our increasingly connected world.

Beyond the classrooms and history books, Tecumseh's impact is felt in the realm of environmental conservation. His profound respect for nature and the belief that the land is something shared by all for survival is a timely reminder of our responsibilities to the planet. Tecumseh saw the earth as a community to which we all belong, a concept that echoes in modern environmental movements that advocate for sustainable living and respect for natural resources.

Today, many environmental groups cite Tecumseh as an inspiration for their efforts to combat pollution, climate change, and habitat destruction. They see his life and teachings as early expressions of ecological wisdom, advocating for a balance between human needs and the health of the planet. Tecumseh's legacy is evident in campaigns that seek to protect forests, rivers, and wildlife—reminding us that, like Tecumseh's time, the land is still a source of life that needs to be respected and preserved.

In addition to inspiring environmentalists, Tecumseh's vision influences current social and political movements. His approach to leadership—emphasizing dialogue, mutual respect, and collective action—is studied by community leaders and activists who work to bring about social change. In a world where conflicts over resources and cultural differences persist, Tecumseh's strategies and his commitment to justice and equity continue to inspire those who strive for a fairer society.

Moreover, Tecumseh's legacy of unity and his fight against the encroachment on Native lands resonate strongly with today's efforts to recognize and rectify historical injustices against Indigenous peoples. His story is often referenced in discussions about land rights and the sovereignty of Native American tribes, providing historical context to the struggles that continue to this day. His life is a call to honor treaties and respect the rights of Indigenous communities, making him a symbol in the ongoing fight for Indigenous rights.

On a broader scale, Tecumseh's influence extends into the arts, where his life and vision have inspired countless works. Filmmakers, novelists, and playwrights have drawn upon his story to explore themes of resistance, leadership, and the clash between different worldviews. These artistic interpretations help keep Tecumseh's memory alive, introducing his character and values to new generations.

Finally, Tecumseh's influence is palpable in the way people today view leadership. His ability to lead with both courage and compassion, to listen earnestly, and to stand firm in his convictions serves as a model for leaders in all fields. From business to politics to community activism, Tecumseh's leadership style—marked by integrity, strategic thinking, and an unwavering commitment to his community—remains relevant.

6 /
learning from tecumseh

key lessons

TECUMSEH'S LIFE is a treasure trove of lessons that can inspire and guide us, even today. Through his experiences, struggles, and successes, he teaches us about courage, leadership, respect, unity, and the importance of our environment. Each of these lessons can help us navigate the challenges we face in our own lives, and they're especially valuable for young minds learning to understand the world.

The Power of Unity

One of Tecumseh's most enduring messages is the importance of unity. He believed that by coming together, people could achieve much more than they could alone. Tecumseh's efforts to unite the Native American tribes showed that even those with different backgrounds and languages could work together toward a common goal. This lesson is crucial in a world where people often focus more on what divides them than on what unites them.

For children, this teaches the value of teamwork and cooperation. Whether it's working on a group project at school, playing a team sport, or helping out in their community, they learn that their actions are stronger when combined with the efforts of others. They also learn that sometimes, like Tecumseh, they might face challenges or disagreements, but through communication and mutual respect, they can overcome these obstacles.

Respect for Nature

Tecumseh's deep connection to the land and his view of it as a shared resource from which all life springs is another profound lesson. He respected nature not only as a source of sustenance but as a sacred space. This respect for the environment is increasingly relevant today as we face environmental challenges like climate change and habitat destruction.

Children can learn from Tecumseh's example to appreciate the natural world around them, understanding that it deserves care and protection. They can engage in activities like recycling, planting trees, or learning about wildlife, which foster an appreciation for the environment and teach them about the impact of their actions on the earth.

Courage and Determination

Tecumseh's life was filled with moments that required immense courage—from leading battles to negotiating with other leaders. His determination in the face of adversity, whether in battle or in his efforts to unite different tribes, shows the importance of standing up for what you believe in, even when it's difficult.

For children, Tecumseh's bravery can be a beacon of inspiration to face their own fears and challenges, whether that means standing up to a bully, trying out for a new activity, or standing up for what is right. Learning about Tecumseh's courage can encourage them to act bravely and persistently in pursuit of their goals.

Leadership with Integrity

Tecumseh was not just a leader in battle; he was a leader in his community. He led with integrity and vision, always with the welfare of his people in mind. He listened to others, was thoughtful in his decisions, and was guided by a strong set of values.

Children learning about Tecumseh's leadership

can see the importance of honesty, integrity, and responsibility. These are qualities that make a true leader, whether one is leading a class project, a sports team, or a group of friends. Understanding the value of good leadership can inspire children to take on leadership roles themselves and to do so with fairness and respect for others.

The Importance of Cultural Heritage

Finally, Tecumseh's life teaches us about the importance of understanding and preserving cultural heritage. He fought not just for land, but for the cultural survival of his people, emphasizing the importance of traditions and knowledge passed down through generations.

This lesson can help children appreciate their own backgrounds and those of others in a more meaningful way. It can encourage them to learn more about their own family histories and to respect the diverse cultures and traditions they encounter in others. This understanding can lead to a richer, more respectful interaction with the world around them.

reflective questions

Upon examining the life and legacy of Tecumseh, it is evident that Tecumseh's narrative is not simply a tale of days long gone, but is also a story rife with ideas and values that resonate today. For young hearts and minds searching for a way to relate to historical figures like Tecumseh with an eye to how they can apply the lessons to their own lives, here are thought-provoking questions to help them situate Tecumseh's metanarrative within their own experience and find ways to apply Tecumseh's lessons such as those of respect for nature, unity, courage in the face of adversity, leadership, and connection to culture to their own lives.

Understanding Unity

1. What does unity mean to you?

- Think about a time when you worked together with others to achieve something. How did teamwork help you succeed?

2. Can you think of a situation at school or in your community where working together might solve a problem?

- What steps would you take to get everyone working together, and how would you handle disagreements?

3. Why do you think Tecumseh wanted different tribes to unite? How can we apply this idea to our world today?

- Consider how people from different backgrounds can come together for a common cause in your community or school.

Respecting Nature

4. What are some ways you can help take care of the environment around you?

- Discuss things you can do at home or school to make a positive impact on nature, like recycling or saving water.

5. Why do you think Tecumseh believed the land was so important?

- How does taking care of the earth help us and future generations?

6. What is your favorite part of nature, and why do you think it's important to protect it?

- Share your thoughts on what makes the natural world special and worth preserving.

Showing Courage

7. What does being brave mean to you?

- Can you think of a time when you had to be brave? What did you do, and how did it make you feel afterward?

8. Tecumseh faced many challenges. What can we learn from how he handled difficult situations?

- Consider what you can do when you face something challenging at school, in sports, or with friends.

9. How can standing up for what you believe make a difference?

- Think about what matters to you and how you can support those beliefs in your everyday life.

Leading with Integrity

10. What qualities do you think make a good leader?

- Reflect on the leaders you know or have read about, including Tecumseh. What makes them good leaders?

11. If you were leading a team project at school, how would you use Tecumseh's lessons to guide your group?

- Think about how you can encourage teamwork, make fair decisions, and help everyone feel included.

12. Why is it important for a leader to listen to others?

- Discuss how listening can help solve problems and make everyone feel important.

Preserving Cultural Heritage

13. What are some traditions in your family or community that are important to you?

- Share why these traditions matter and how they help you understand your heritage.

14. How can learning about different cultures and traditions make us better people?

- Consider what you can learn from others and how respecting diverse cultures can lead to a more harmonious community.

15. Why did Tecumseh fight so hard to preserve his people's way of life?

- Think about what you would want to protect about your own culture or community and why.

additional materials

glossary

Alliance

Definition: An agreement between two or more parties, made to advance common goals and to secure common interests.

In Context: Tecumseh formed alliances with various tribes and sometimes with the British to strengthen his position against American settlers.

Confederacy

Definition: A union of different groups, states, or tribes who come together for a common purpose, maintaining their own individual leadership.

In Context: Tecumseh worked hard to build a

confederacy of Native American tribes to resist the expansion of European settlers.

Culture

Definition: The ideas, customs, social behaviors, and traditions of a particular group of people or society.

In Context: Tecumseh fought not only to protect his people's land but also to preserve their culture and traditions.

Diplomacy

Definition: The art of managing international relations, typically by a country's representatives abroad. It can also refer to skill in handling affairs without arousing hostility.

In Context: Tecumseh used diplomacy to negotiate with other tribes and with the British to gain support for his cause.

Heritage

Definition: The traditions, achievements, beliefs, etc., that are part of the history of a group or nation.

In Context: Tecumseh's dedication to defending his people's heritage was a central part of his leadership and legacy.

Integrity

Definition: The quality of being honest and having strong moral principles.

In Context: Tecumseh is remembered for his integrity, both in his personal character and in his leadership.

Leadership

Definition: The action of leading a group of people or an organization.

In Context: Tecumseh is celebrated for his leadership skills, particularly in building a coalition of tribes and leading them in resistance against American forces.

Negotiation

Definition: Discussion aimed at reaching an agreement.

In Context: Tecumseh often engaged in negotiations with other tribal leaders and European powers as he sought to secure a future for his people.

Sovereignty

Definition: Supreme power or authority, such as that held by a state or a monarch. For tribal nations, it refers to the right to govern themselves.

In Context: A significant part of Tecumseh's mission was to preserve the sovereignty of Native American tribes against U.S. governmental policies and settlement.

Treaty

Definition: A formally concluded and ratified agreement between countries or groups.

In Context: Tecumseh opposed many treaties made between Native American tribes and the United States because he felt they were unfair and harmful to his people.

Unity

Definition: The state of being united or joined as a whole.

In Context: Unity was a cornerstone of Tecumseh's strategy, as he believed that only by coming together could the Native American tribes resist the settlers effectively.

Visionary

Definition: A person with original ideas about what the future will or could be like.

In Context: Tecumseh was considered a visionary for his plans to unite the Native American tribes and for his foresight into the challenges and opportunities his people would face.

These terms are like tools in a toolbox—each one has its own use and importance. By understanding these words, you can better grasp the complex ideas they represent and see how they fit into the bigger story of Tecumseh's life and legacy. Just like Tecumseh brought together different tribes, understanding these key terms brings together different parts of his story, helping you see the full picture of who he was and what he stood for.

timeline

Early Life

   - 1768: Tecumseh is born near the Scioto River, in what is now Ohio. He is born into the Shawnee tribe during a period of great upheaval, as European settlers are increasingly encroaching on Native American lands.

Formative Years

   - 1774: The Battle of Point Pleasant, an early and significant clash between American colonists and Native Americans, occurs. Although Tecumseh is very young, the battle has a lasting impact on his people and contributes to his early awareness of the settlers' threat.

- 1779: During Tecumseh's childhood, his father is killed by white settlers. This event profoundly influences his view of the settlers and starts to shape his resolve to protect his people and their way of life.

Rise to Leadership

- 1791: The Battle of the Wabash (also known as St. Clair's Defeat) sees a confederation of Native tribes achieve a significant victory against the United States. Tecumseh is not yet a chief but is growing in prominence among his people.

- 1794: The Battle of Fallen Timbers results in Native American defeat; Tecumseh, who did not participate, is critical of the tribes who signed the Treaty of Greenville the following year, ceding much territory to the U.S. This further cements his desire to resist American expansion.

Building the Confederacy

- 1805: Tecumseh's brother, Tenskwatawa, known as the Prophet, has a series of visions, leading to the founding of Prophetstown in Indiana. This town becomes a cultural and religious center for Tecumseh's movement.

- 1809: Tecumseh travels extensively to recruit allies among the Native tribes. His charisma and diplomatic skill help him to form a broad confederation against American expansion.

The War of 1812

- 1811: Battle of Tippecanoe: While Tecumseh is away seeking further alliances, U.S. forces led by William Henry Harrison attack Prophetstown. The town is destroyed, seriously undermining Tecumseh's confederacy.

- 1812: The War of 1812 begins between the United States and Britain. Tecumseh aligns with the British, seeing an opportunity to curb American expansion. His forces play a key role in several battles.

- 1813: Battles of Fort Meigs and the Thames: Tecumseh's forces are involved in the siege of Fort Meigs. Later, at the Battle of the Thames in October, Tecumseh is killed, dealing a devastating blow to his confederation and the Native American resistance.

Legacy

- Post-1813: Following Tecumseh's death, his vision of a united Native resistance dwindles. However, his legacy of leadership, vision, and resistance to dispossession continues to inspire subsequent generations.

Modern Recognition

- Throughout the 19th and 20th centuries: Tecumseh becomes a legendary figure in American and Native American history. He is remembered in various ways, including in books, movies, and as a symbol of resistance and unity.

- 21st century: Tecumseh's strategies and leadership are studied in military and academic circles. His commitment to unity and justice influences contemporary discussions about cultural preservation and the rights of indigenous peoples.

further reading/resources

Educational Websites

3. National Museum of the American Indian (NMAI) (website: americanindian.si.edu)

- Operated by the Smithsonian Institution, NMAI provides a wealth of information about Native American history and cultures. Their online resources include digital exhibits, videos, and educational materials that cover a wide range of topics, including leaders like Tecumseh.

4. PBS Learning Media (website: pbslearningmedia.org)

- PBS offers a variety of resources for students and teachers, including documentaries and interactive lessons about Native American history. Their collection includes materials specifically about Tecumseh and the War of 1812, which can help students visualize and understand the historical context.

Interactive and Multimedia Resources

5. "Tecumseh's Vision" – Part of the 'We Shall Remain' Series (website: pbs.org/wgbh/americanexperience/films/tecumseh/)

- This documentary is part of PBS's acclaimed 'American Experience' series and provides an in-depth look at Tecumseh's life and the formidable coalition he built against American expansion.

6. Native Knowledge 360° (website: americanindian.si.edu/nk360)

- This initiative by the National Museum of the American Indian provides students and educators with new perspectives on Native American history and cultures. It offers a range of multimedia resources that are both informative and engaging.

Local and Community Resources

Visit Local Museums and Cultural Centers

- Many regions, especially those rich in Native American history, have local museums and cultural centers that offer workshops, exhibits, and presentations about the local tribes and figures like Tecumseh. These can be great for immersive learning experiences.

Library Programs

- Check out your local library's events calendar. Many libraries host Native American Heritage Month activities, storytelling sessions, and history talks that can provide valuable insights into Tecumseh's era and the broader aspects of Native American cultures.

closing

A Leader for All Times

Tecumseh was a leader who stood out not only because of his skill as a warrior but because of his ability to inspire and unite people. His dream of bringing together different Native American tribes was revolutionary at the time. He saw the power of unity in a way that was ahead of his era. Today, we live in a world that is more connected than ever, yet we often find ourselves divided. Tecumseh's message about the strength in unity is as important now as it was then. It teaches us that by working together, we can overcome challenges much bigger than ourselves.

Visionary in Action

What makes Tecumseh's story particularly compelling is how he turned his vision into action.

He didn't just dream about unity; he traveled vast distances, speaking to different tribes, sharing his vision, and facing countless challenges. His proactive approach teaches us the importance of not just having ideas but putting them into action. For young readers like you, this can be a powerful lesson in taking initiative—whether it's standing up for what you believe in, participating in community service, or working on group projects at school.

Respect for Nature

Tecumseh's deep respect for nature and his belief in living harmoniously with the environment is another aspect of his legacy that resonates strongly today. As we face environmental issues such as climate change and habitat destruction, Tecumseh's respect for the earth offers a poignant reminder of the importance of caring for our planet. This can inspire you to engage in activities that protect the environment, learn more about sustainability, and understand how your actions impact the world around you.

Overcoming Adversity

Tecumseh faced significant adversity throughout his life—from losing his father at a young age to battling against the encroachment on his people's lands. His resilience in the face of these challenges shows us the power of perseverance. For anyone facing difficulties, Tecumseh's life is a testament to the fact that while we may not always control what happens to us, we can always choose how to respond. His courage to continue fighting for his beliefs, despite setbacks, is a powerful lesson in resilience and determination.

A Bridge Between Cultures

Finally, Tecumseh's efforts to bridge different cultures and foster understanding among diverse groups highlight his role as a peacemaker. He knew that lasting peace would come not from conflict but through cooperation and mutual respect. This part of his legacy is particularly important today, in a world where we encounter diverse perspectives and backgrounds daily. Tecumseh's life encourages us to learn from each other, respect our differences, and find common ground.

Why Tecumseh Matters Today

So, why does Tecumseh's story matter to you, as a young reader? It matters because it's not just about history; it's about the values and lessons that help us navigate the challenges of today's world. Tecumseh's leadership, vision, and values provide a roadmap for how to live with courage, integrity, and respect for others and the environment.

As you move forward, think of Tecumseh not

just as a figure from the past, but as a source of inspiration for how you can lead, how you can make a difference, and how you can respect and protect the world we all share. Tecumseh's life reminds us that each of us has the potential to make an impact, and that together, we can accomplish incredible things.

Remember, history isn't just about what happened; it's about what we learn from it, and how we use those lessons to shape our future. Tecumseh's story is a shining example of how enduring values can guide us through the complexities of modern life and help us strive for a better world.

www.ingramcontent.com/pod-product-compliance
Lightning Source LLC
Chambersburg PA
CBHW060455160726
47992CB00003B/1221